Rosella

poetry by
Rosella Stern

CHAPBOOKS, BOOKS, POETRY PACKS
AND POEMS PUBLISHED IN ANTHOLOGIES

People's Lives, Honey, People's Lives (circa 1970)
Saying Yes (circa 1975)
Tina Modotti poem (date unknown)
"Yankui Pig Dog Poem" (in *Poetry From Violence* 1976)
Comes November (1993)
The Braid, The Cap of Hair (first printed 1994)
If Not Now: West Coast Poems (copyright 2012)
Preliminary Kaddish (copyright 2015)
52 Pickup: A Pack of Poems (copyright 2020)

Rosella
Rosella Stern
All rights reserved
All contents copyright 2025
ISBN: 978-0-9833498-8-4
Published by Cygnet Press
Design and layout: Tim Anderson/Paula Donahue
Editor: Paula Donahue

FOREWARD

This small collection of Rosella Stern's many poems has seven sections organized by theme. Some were previously published, others found in folders, boxes, hand-written on yellow legal pads, and on scraps of paper. Because she wrote poetry for 60 years, the style and formatting changed over time and differ from poem to poem within each section of the book. Her daughter Rebecca Bloom has given permission to publish any or all of it.

The book is titled *Rosella* because the poems reveal a bit of who she was, but the seven sections do not reveal her complete person. She was incredibly witty and sometimes, hilariously funny, sometimes a little wild, but always concerned about making her home a retreat for herself and others. She cared deeply about human rights and helped many individuals in so many ways.

These poems reveal how she felt about writing, her memories of her past, her Jewish identity, her connection to nature, her loves, her losses, and her resilience.

Hopefully, this sampling of her poetry will engross you.

ACKNOWLEDGMENTS

Several readers helped me decide how to assemble this book after choosing the poems from Rosella's vast collection.

Thanks to Kim Vivier who used her editorial skills to make suggestions, Lauren Marble who read the poems as a poet herself, Judy Kistler-Robinson and Kate Hildebrand who read the poems with the eyes of voracious readers, and Kate Harrington who read with her experience as an author.

Thanks especially to Tim Anderson for working closely with me on this project.

Thanks to you all for helping me send more of my sister's poems out into the world.

Sincerely,
Paula Donahue

DEDICATION

For Rosella's daughter, Rebecca Bloom
and grandchild, Eli Bloom.
She deeply loved them both.

CONTENTS

ON WRITING

"I know
I have been
writing the blues
and singing them."
(Poems from the 70s)

Gimme a Chunka Thick White Paper

Gimme a chunka thick white paper
I'm gonna write me out a poem
in black in big letters with fat lines
man, it's gonna be the
heaviest poem
to come off the line in years.

These Poems!

These poems!
They have become like children.
They cling to me
waiting for their noses to be wiped.
They need their commas tucked in
They need their bottoms pulled up.
They are incorrigible –
I have been training them to sleep all night,
but often, about midnight, when I am about to wash,
or think over tomorrow's supper,
They beg me, in their charming way,
to turn all my undivided attention to them.
And, when I think I've kicked the
very last one out of the nest
and turned my back, momentarily,
on them all,
Here comes another,
Kicking,
and crying to be born.

Comes November

The nights' dark fluids
are seeing the light of day.
Now some mornings are made
entirely of coffee, India ink and blood.
The fluids exchange with a prayer or curse,
such as the hour and day allow.

Comes November
and the day races on
or stands dead in its tracks.
Coffee runs me along reason's jagged edge.
Dark permanent ink outlines the image.
I declare my own reality.

The words take shape as the day does.
I name and name and name,
saying that litany long
after the sky becomes the same
indelible purple
the pen holds.

The deepest colors come on now
following the year's narrow arc.
There is some comfort
in how they are like
winter earth, like henna, like fur,
all a little red at the center.

And when there is no ink
and yet a need to write
the word that is to a sound
as a wound is to a breath

I take the pen deep,
reaching the heart's blood.

For to name my own small truth
I take whatever is at hand —
dull instrument, sharpened stone,
my own hand
smeared with my own blood.

For I have learned to let blood
and still sustain my life.
I cannibal the fluids
Coffee to ink to blood to ink.
In such darkness I've become
a clever robber of the heart.

Psalms for Today

The Israeli woman
Did not understand
When the translator
Tried to tell her

I was a poet
"What is poetry?"
She asked in Hebrew
And I could not reply
Not knowing the new Hebrew
Myself — so I tried again

The translator said
"It rhymes."
And I said, "No
Not necessarily."

So, I tried again
I thought slowly
And I said
"Songs without music."

"Oh," the translator said
"That's good. Did you
Think of that yourself?"
Then the Israeli woman
Rounded her eyes saying
"Yes."

Later I thought
I should have said
"Like psalms
but for today."

A Thought So Grievous

Once I thought a thought
So grievous
That it destroyed my belly
Lay heavy
On my brain

Was it as terrible and destroying
As Darwin imagining
The devious origin of the species
Against all the beliefs
Of his house, his pious wife
His English culture

Was it as defying as Moses
His mouth full of hesitation
Defying Pharaoh
To set his people free

Like that?
Like Olivier cowed by
Shakespearean beauty
Streisand unable to sing
For others for money

No nothing like that
Just awareness
Of the power of my own words
When on the page
No longer in the mind
No longer in the mouth
Just the power of words

What the Old Man Told Me

This is what the old man told me
Not all at once but over time
And it becomes true again
In the telling

In the time it takes
To become a beloved
Not just a lover
Not simply the other

What he said
Becomes truer in the telling
And I tell it to you again
To believe it myself

Something about being
Because the truth is
The doing of it
Not the telling

Yet for me
Being who I am
Telling is a kind
Of doing

One O'Clock Revision

The day rushes on
To a standstill
Clock straight up
I eat my 3 o'clock snack
At noon
Hungry and unsatisfied

Get the papers
Way before dawn
Read everything
Before the mandatory
9 o'clock call
Across the states

Think of everyone
I miss and love
Before 10
Dishes done
Bed made
Red paisley winter cover
Rediscovered from a pile

Hair a red for winter
Washed, dried, bent under
As a stick is bent
As I am bent
Half-past, three quarters gone
Tired beyond speech

Now a quarter after

Poetry in Motion

I went to the edge of the abyss
and I laughed the laugh
of centuries
golden light all visible around me

I walked on the other side
the dark side
and I came back
simpler than before

You wouldn't know this
to see me
to look at me in passing
I look like some older woman
out shopping for shoes

I look like some woman in jeans
walking through the
vegetables at Whole Foods
fingering the carrots for luck
and the avocados for sensuality.

How could you know?

REMEMBERING

"I can hold memories within me like eggs."
(from a scrap of paper in Rosella's office)

The Snow Prince

— For My Father, Dead a Dozen Years

The snow prince walks in the door
All snow at the edges,
Trimming thin, dark overcoat
And younger than my heart can bear.
My father, thin as a sapling
Leans over my crib, before I can speak his name.
Cold breathes from his pores.
He has walked from the bus
And the snow makes a little stream
Of flakes around and towards me
As he bends over me
Handing me all his love
In a box of dresses made of ruffles
Top to bottom.
All the love I need is in the snow
On his fedora
And the epaulets of snow on each shoulder,
Badges of honor from his day away.
I love him.
He is so young in my memory
And not yet gone to war.

Years later, in the store
He unfurls the colored silks of the trade
That fall in billows and make elegant banners
And butterfly wings of color
Out across the measuring tables.
My love flies out to him, yet unspoken on my lips
In the middle of the store
On a Saturday afternoon in the Midwest

And the salesgirls measure out
The silks and woolens and the cottons
Are folded back in sensible folds
Across the boards.

Later still, his hands knot
And cannot hold the club, the bat, the slippery silk
All that he loved, with ease.
The heart knots, it cannot hold its love,
With ease.
It beats a hard race in his chest
Faster than he can run.

His beauty becomes a mask,
Even in life.
His mouth gapes, opening in silence
As he sleeps,
Saying death death death.
The good prince has gone dead asleep
Heart in mouth, clubs propped against the chair
Dancing slippers flung off
Against the edge of the bed.
The good prince has gone dead asleep
And I did not say goodbye
So as he would notice.

I wear a star some days
To remember him in honor
And I wear color some days
To remember his love
And some days
I wear black.

Tending Beauty
— the rose and the thorn

She was poisoned
For wanting beauty
She was pained
By the woodiness of canes
And hooked deep,
Once in the bone.

Mother said
"You'll pay for this.
You'll pay for color
For the softness
Of a petal
Mottled like watered silk.

You'll see blackness
For the desire of color.
You'll know pain
For the pleasure
Of flowers

You'll be your
Father's daughter
Hungering after beauty
Won't you, aren't you
Your father's daughter?"

Our Mother's Daughters

Well, we are all just that,
aren't we, our mother's daughters.
Our own faces in death
will be like theirs
as in birth we are theirs.
Our breathing is a memory
of their breath.

We are that flesh and blood,
body and memory
tied to each other
as to oxygen or music
for necessity
and to the heart as it speeds
and slows.

God listens to what
we know in our hearts
and dare not say.
God asks in our own voice,
"Say something, before I leave."
"What do you want to hear?"
He answers in our mother's voice.

And we answer back,
generation to generation,
say, "I love you."
We will miss you always
as we miss you
now,
even before death.

For Buby
—Eulogy

There is that thread that runs so true
From her to you, me to thee
All of us, I and Thou.

She found us a country.
She gave us a space inside a great city.
She let us know, each of us
That we could make it again
In our own image, as the years roll away.

Some of us she named.
Some of us she made who we are.
She called out our names,
Cautioned us, fed us,
Made us see, even as she no longer could.

Some she gave life.
Some she showed the pride of work well done,
What to do with ten golden fingers,
How to stand firm
How to survive
Despite all, everything.

And how to carry the work you must do
And your family, in your own hands.

She held us with her plain power.
We use our hands as she needed to, and her in image.
We direct our spirit, remembering her soul.

She made of us a tribe.
And we stand in her circle.
And we will miss her and bless her memory
And carry her within our hearts
Until we and our children and our children's children
In all those generations
Are gone.

Cutting Bread

Sometimes I need to cut rough bread.
I hold the bread between my breasts,
another breast, a third breast,
baked dark brown on weekdays,
braided golden for the Sabbath.

I take the heavy knife in my small hand
like a scythe
to cut a swath of bread
a great round of bread
always aiming the knife point
toward my heart, where it stays
as the bread turns 'round it.
I carve a good slice, a peasant slice,
as my grandma did and did.

I'll put *schmaltz* on it.
I'll put butter on it — and salt.
I'll find a garden radish for a spice
and be home again within my heart.

Forgive me. I have no words now
for what I do.
I am ignorant in more than one language.
What was my Buby's word for bread?
Broit? Khleb?
She cut a *schtikle* from the loaf.
What is the word here for heart? For salt?
What is the name of memory?

lt is winter
and I am having Russian dreams again.
I stand in a place I never knew. Knowing.
Late afternoons,
forced by a certain slant of grey light,
I cook beet soup, *borscht*,
stirring with hands much larger than my own

Backyard Shadow

Didn't know I lived in a tenement
Until later
Didn't know I was poor
Paycheck to paycheck poor
Did you?

Didn't know grandma fed me lunch
Because my mom couldn't.
Wouldn't give me peanut butter
White bread
Too American for the immigrant's daughter.

Didn't know the shadows at the corners
Were formed by other people's
Little spaces thought they were,
But couldn't be sure.
Never saw the inside
Where the other children slept
In closet bedrooms
Or stacked along the walls,
Two high three together
Crowded by shadows
Of each other's lives.

Didn't realize how many
Lived with grandmas
Their moms gone mad or disappeared
During the war
Didn't know
That the smell was someone
Else's cooking and sweat
From the factory night job.
Didn't know, couldn't be sure.

Backyard Girls

Childhood's soft edge
remembering the girls
of my apartment yard
varied and hidden
eager or afraid
unformed yet for what
they would become

Myrna, luxuriant
red hair Raphaelesque
at 11, a little beyond us
yet she slept in a pull out
closet bed with her brother, 8,
can radiance come from that?

And Fern had only
her grandma for comfort
in the war years
twirling her story
all sing song in the courtyard
what was she telling

Linda so fat of face
only a mother could love
and didn't
already peripheral
out of sight right there
facing the alley

Claudine
the janitor's daughter
a Christian among Jews
lapsed Catholic, recent Lutheran
believing, lighting the tree
pinking off the Christmas ravioli

Sheila up other stairs
with her dog like Lassie
in such a little place
no room to run
up from the bus stop
on the boulevard below
A movie star face among us

occasionally Susan below me
with her brother
brilliant and ignored back then
only much later to become
what she was meant to be
and be it fully, revealed

someone died
a cousin who had lived
near the end of the row
leukemia, they said
one among the others
who went too young
no one saved, how could they

and me, sandwiched in
between floors
between neighbors
heard, hardly seen

me screaming quietly,
to get out, remaining impatient
in my mind, there, in the room

Adrienne, my friend
I listened with you
through the wall
like a sister, dressed
like me me like you
70 years on I still know
where you are and how you are

A blessing.

YIDDISH SOUL

"Ich gehaben ein dybbuk"
The crazy spirit is in me, on me
Do I like it?
I'm carrying it, ain't I?"
(*Seven Yiddish Curses for Today*)

If I Believe

— at the Jewish New Year

Some by fire, some by air, no air, air.
Some by air being captured in trees, tossed.
Some by water and what came with it.
Some poisoned, filled, floated away, bloated.
Some by mouths filled with mud and words unsaid.
Some by stoning, by cars, walls of buildings.

When the earth moves, we are moved with it,
some by force, being dragged to sea
or out in it floating
on a wave not understood.

Inscribe me, Oh God,
another year, another.
Forgive me my sins
against myself, against others.
Forgive me, forgive me.
Observe me in the act of such forgiving.
Forgive me, don't forgive me,
but forgive my children
or the world's children and my children's children.
Is all this forgiveness not well spent
in a time of darkness
and the hope of a new beginning?

The Eight Ways of Giving
— *when a man who has nothing gives to a man with less*

His voice is wider than the walls.
He speaks his truth
and hears no other.
Deafness falls around him,
making his personal darkness more opaque.
And he sits in it.

On nights like this
he is not his mother's son.
There is no bed waiting for him,
there is only this floor, small.
And he will sleep on it.

His own bigness is an intrusion,
to be stepped over,
stepped around. There is no ignoring him.

Everything that can be done for a human
must be done for him
as a mother would.
Feed him, help him wash,
cut his hair, trim his nails, his beard.
Sit him down before you
and shape the heap
into a semblance of a man again,
man to man,
but gently.

There are said to be eight ways of giving.

There is the giving to the person
who knows he is the receiver, you the giver.
There is the giving when you receive thanks.
And there is the giving when you
receive no thanks.
There is the giving when your charity
comes from the soul
and no one but you
knows that you have given.
And so on.

Nathaniel sits in your room.
His cry for help is a pattern on the walls.
The sound becomes dirty, it obliterates
what small things you have.
Yet, everything must be given that can be given
clean shirt, clean hands,
meat and the way to cut meat,
water and the cup to drink it from,
money and the way to spend it.
The hand is cupped upward,
endlessly.
He asks.
He asks.

And you want to give
and you want to stop it,
the Asking.
You want to say "No" to Nathaniel in the room,
but not in anger.

You want to say "No" from a deep necessity
that is beyond despair.
"Leave my floor. Leave my small room.

Find another way.
Reach your own bottom, alone.
Wear my pants, my shirt,
put my food in your belly.
Now go!"

There are eight ways of giving.
Is one to say "No"
to the need that cannot be denied.
to the need that has Death
as its second face?

Prohibitions Sacred and Profane

Do not weave together linen and silk
Do not covet thy neighbor's spouse
Do not cook the calf in its mother's milk
Do not wear shoes in a house of mourning
Do not bow down again to golden idols

Do not and do not and do not and do not

Do not wear a blonde wig or false mustache
and pretend to be another
Do not now or have ever been
a member of the Communist party
Do not bear false witness in a court of law
Do not have your mother cheat for you
Do not forget the six million who have died
Or the one million or the others now forgotten
Or the most of millions dying now

Do not let the flag touch the ground

The Sweet Smoke of Prayer

Don't worry the details
The dots above the vowel
The lines below
Go beyond the trope you know
Let the thought fly up
Release the letters
From the page
Release the sorrow
From the heart
Make gladness

We have nothing but ourselves now
Not bull blood
Not the warm blood of sheep
On the temple altar
Only sacrifice on the altar of ourselves
Purified or sullied
By the art of living
Made ready for this
Made of bones and flesh
Yet in your image

We ignite our hearts
With prayer
We ask forgiveness
We pray for rain
In a dry season of the soul
We pray for dry
In a wet season
Of confusion near madness
Then we are released
From self to self
As the candle makes smoke
From wick to fire

Fearing the Smallest of Small Things

Sand
Dust
Lint

The dead skin we shed
The dust mites that eat it

Fuzz from dandelions
Oh dog dander
And tiny tree pollen
Each spring like now

The motes in your eyes
Those black dots you see
Crossing the eye's private horizon

Now Lord help me
You us all
The white blood cells
The plasma that fights the virus
There being nothing else
Whether home alone
Or out

In a season of prayer
Shall we?

Need to Breathe
— on reading High Holiday Prayer Book

When I think on these things,
I feel bonds of tightness in my chest
And a twisting in my gut.

The chakras are in a knot.
Breathe me out of this!

Biblical Magic

Water to wine
Wine to water
When you need that

Sea to land
Land to sea
When you're not careful

Sticks to snakes
Snakes to sticks
When they're in your house

Bread to body
Bread as bread
When you're hungry

Self unaware
To naked self
When you know

Hate to love
Love to universal love
Love precious love

Transmigration
Of self
Of souls

Sela

Seven Yiddish Curses for Today

1. *"Ach cholerea!"*
It's terrible, so terrible,
Like cholera, or the Black Death
If it's still around.
My advice, take 2 aspirin, or a glass of tea
With a little honey and lemon.

2. *"The handz, der foos, Alles felt nicht gut!"*
I ache from head to toe
Do you care? Of course not!
You should live so long
To know such pain!

3. *"Gey hock ein chinick."*
Go hit a tea kettle,
You useless thing
with an empty head!

4. (In English)
"You can't sit on two stools
with one *tuchas*."
Hey, stop fucking around,
We're on to you!

5. *"Zol er krenken en gedenken"*
Let him suffer and remember.
This means you, mister.

6. *"Ich gehaban ein dybbuk"*
The crazy spirit is in me, on me
Do I like it?
I'm carrying it, ain't I?

7. *"Gey en dr'ert":*
Go to hell!
And on the way back
Bring me a bagel with
Smear, and an egg cream.

LOVE AND LOSS

"Do not think of sorrow
as an empty hole.
It is only half that."
(Sorrow's Half)

The Dying Heart

we will beat out a poem
from our sorrow
like the beat of your dying heart
sometimes faster than a runner
sometimes slow
hardly there

we beat it, we beat out the rhythm
a metronome of the dying heart
the maker of rhythm
that cannot be saved
and the man who no longer
wants to save it

so tired from the race
so tired, again at peace, he says
as, perhaps, I am not
not yet able to be at peace
marking as I am the beating
marking it off

Sorrow's Half

do not think of sorrow
as an empty hole
it is only half that
you the bean-shaped remnant
of what was
and you are here, still here
to mourn the emptiness
perhaps before it is fully empty
merely a remembrance
of the future alone

Shoes and Paperwork

shoes and paperwork
are not
what you were made of
so I cannot do that work
just now
you were hats and the blues
well, that's not entirely true
you were some shoes
red Coogies bought
for early father's day
Florsheims for weddings
and funerals
but not your own
you wore no shoes
only a shroud
and shrunken cheeks
that were your own leather
of worn skin sunken low
forgive me
when I cannot do
the work just now
of shoes and paperwork
only sort the blues
celebrate the hats

The Absence of Blackness

the absence of his blackness
does not bring more light
only a darker hue
as indigo is to blue
darker, a more natural shade
the essence of the blues itself

the absence of his blackness
is the loss of his radiance
eyes alight with private knowing
polished brown skin
on a perfectly smooth
well-shaped skull, shining

the absence of his blackness
is the loss of chest tones
musical speech as suggested song
rhythm that is a heart beat
a personal dance, glorious
yet irregular, fluttering

the absence of his blackness
is the loss of laughter
when there is no joke told
only life lived together
as call and response

The Anatomy of Tears

I cannot explain
the anatomy of tears
when I have none

I know that water
is inherently a crystal
and so tears must be
when they come
when they come

consciousness creates all
it creates sadness
without tears
if that is what is required

some water on earth
is older than the sun, heavier
twice as heavy as hydrogen
these must be the hidden
tears l feel
behind the dry gladness

Future Nostalgia

future nostalgia
is the arbiter
of my goals

I long for what is next
as though it has already happened
I miss it with an ache
around the soul like nausea
existential, yet physical
covered over, just so
by the paper of my skin
an origami box of the self
self-made

goodbye tomorrow
I wave at a doppelganger
that is me, shrunken and old
as the sound of memory
goes down another octave
ding, ding, ding,
like a train that has just passed

Ain't Gonna Use Black Magic on It

Ain't gonna use black magic on it.
Not worth the trouble
don't want to win no hearts
ain't worth the bother
don't want to drag home no dead meat
old memories, somebody else's love.

Ain't gonna use black magic on it.
Ain't gonna wage no war
won't have no battles in the night
can't have no troubles in my mind
no covers in the air
no kisses aimed at winning you.

No sweet man, this is lasting peace,
No wild Indian love, *amor Indio*,
no lovers' blows in the night.
You can put your mind to rest
you can put your heart to sleep.
It's all quiet now, go easy.

Ain't gonna use black magic on it.
Don't want to win what isn't given
don't want to do more than
walk up near that line.
Lord have mercy,
don't want to cross that line.

Don't want to be in no one's space.
This is not Red Rover,
ain't comin' over to get
your soul, forget it.
Ain't comin over,
the door is closed, I'm home alone.

Ain't gonna use black magic on it.
Did that once
got what I wanted.
Look what's it's done to me now.
Taken me years to recover,
truth be told, ain't over it yet.

Maybe I never will.
Like the man says,
can't always want what you get.
Got to go easy with this magic shit.
Someone tell you the truth
in another language, you better listen up.

But I ain't gonna use black magic on it.
When a man says no to someone's soul
best thing to do is walk.
Maybe come back in a while,
Say, "Let's be friends."
Say, "Let's have lunch."
Never say, no, never say again.

"I know the color of our laugh" or
"Your feet are older than your hands,"
Never say,
"I felt your mind, I held it in my hands."
No, never say that again, Ain't no fool.
A girl's only human.

Got to keep on down the road,
keep on walking, even if you crawl.

Ain't gonna use black magic on it.
'Less I have to.

Him

Of course Him
Him him him
Taken away

Another year comes 'round
A year without madness
Not even my own

A year without tears
Yet filled with sorrow
Dawn awake again

Not about him
All about him
About us all

Those we are missing
Wrists without hands
Nothing to touch

Glass Can Cut Glass

The glass man holds a mirror
to my heart.
How could it be otherwise?
The reflection of just the corner
of his eye was sunlight for me.

And there I am again,
foolish, intrepid,
pressing my nose against the pane
wanting to smell and taste,
but that's just the thing
about glass,
it preserves, it protects,
it tries to hold the heat away.

The legend says the French thought
citrus oil rubbed on the outside
of the goblet would change the taste
of what's within.
They didn't understand the nature of glass
Then again, there is the possibility
of permeability everywhere,
isn't there?

And glass can cut glass.

What is Air

It hurts so
To look out the back window now
For some trees are silver
Some have turned to acid green
And all are shaking their heads,
Such untamed women.

Have you all done
What you said?
Have you all done
What you set out to do?
You had better.

For you are dead now who could
Sing an angry red song.
Fling death around you
Like a cape.
My father is dead now
Who died caught up on his own hook.

Beautiful fish, arched out of water.
His father is dead
That old man who could have fathered
Again enough children to march
Small platoons behind him
To his grave.

Have you all done
What you said?
Have you all done
What you set out to do?
You had better.

For what is air
That shakes the trees
Like so much hair
And cannot fill
Your closed lungs
With song?

Do You Know Darkness?

It is the place behind my heart
where no light sings
and the breath moves through
as in a reed
but there is no melody.

Do you remember stillness?
It is the moment when love leaves —
the heart shudders, ceases its rhythm.
It is as though the hummingbird
stopped still, hung in air mid-flight.

Do you recall
the road back to living?
It is a step of radiance
as moving toward the full moon
when it glows between
the notch of two dark hills.
It is the light from flat cheekbones
and jewel-like eyes
of women who have given birth
to themselves.

Do you yearn for the future
still having nostalgia for the past?
It is all one thing, really,
that we long for.
It is the memory of what is to come.
The light beyond the darkness,
the breath that sings in the reed.

Red Wagon

No meaning but in things, he said.
Objectify the soul, they said.
Speak only of the little red wagon
streaked with rain,
streaked with rain,
and not the heart.

I go out now
looking for something
to carry my heart around,
knowing no little red wagon
can do the job.
For being this heavy

what my heart needs now
is a van. More than a van,
it needs a sixteen-wheeler to cart it.
I mean a rig. Something that uses diesel
pulls up at truck stops and
likes to chow down on grits, home fries,
calls the other guys, "Good buddy."

What other vehicle could schlep
my heart around now?
Do I need a hearse, a tow truck?
Triple A knows what I need,
but does anyone respond to this
emergency call?

I thought I had 24-hour service.
I thought I had insurance
against being left stranded
on the side of the road —
beach side, riverside, mountainside, 2 a.m.

Okay, I'll objectify my heart,
I'll put it out there
disguised as a landscape.
No more talk about the soul in search
No more talk about the heart longing.
Objectify, I say, objectify I will.

I'll say red sails.
I'll say blue moon.
I'll say yellow rose,
no mauve desire.
But the picture doesn't come up
in color.

And the heart remains
heavy, red.
And the call goes out again
the call goes out,
"Red wagon.
Red wagon."

OBSERVATIONS

"And the poetry hawk,
sharp eyed,
circles round."
(*The Hawks*)

The Mystery of the Ordinary

first the dragonflies
then the butterflies
crowds of white moths
compared to angel's wings
the geckos, always
colored like trees, like the house
green as grass

and the squirrels circling
the limbs of trees, continuously
like foxtails on the shoulders
of an elegant, elderly woman

The Hawks

ahead, always just ahead
and above
the hawks be circling, circling
over the river at the tree line,
over the highway, near the crossroad
over the street, urban, unexpected
they be circling, lazy loops, lazy loops

as I go down to sleep
the hawks of memory
and the hawks of dreams
be circling, circling,
they follow each other 'round
and just behind the thought beyond
reach a kind of prey of the mind,
they be circling, circling

and the poetry hawk
sharp-eyed,
circles round

The Crows Will Have a Use For It

Do you have something to discard today
Last year's unused telephone book
A broken mug, old jewelry
Hair from your brush?
Toss it out the door
The crows will build
A village in the sky with it

Do you have anger you can't say
A sorrow that eats your heart in quiet
Something to tell the neighbors
About their dog, their middle child?
Think it again near the window
The crows will have a name for it
Shouting it back and forth
Across the gulley or the street

Did you see the baby eagle dead
The raccoon frozen on the lawn
The jay squawking, losing the battle?
Fear for them
The crows have gone to war with all
To win

Just at twilight above the bridge
Nearing home
Did you feel the crows fill the sky
Making it blacker with wing tips and heads
Than the night to come?
Then you know for certain
The river water isn't yours
Your house is owned by them
And the trees all around
And the street where they strut

A Minyan of Ibis

I hadn't asked for this
Not a murder of crows
But a convocation
A minyan of ibis
A dozen or just less
Ten for prayer
Pecking the earth
In search of truth
All clustered in creamy feathers
At the river and then nearby

They walk the earth again
Still in search of their god
Tiny yet secure on wide feet
Crescent bills arced
Single file marched
Aimed intentional

I know them now
As I did then
In Egypt

Tell me what has changed

Orion

Just last night
Orion lay above
The ocean
Sword and all
Belt wrapped
Around his waist
Studded with stars

Isn't it wonderful
Ocean and sky
So full of stars
And the pictures
That stars make
Of themselves
Named and remembered
Now a thousand thousand
Years from then
A billion billion

Be thankful for this
So casually seen
Driving home

Then Venus
The morning star

Southern Birds

Egrets and great blue herons
White owls with barred faces
All or most of the exotics
Sure I know them
Can name them
Most of them

But when I know the name
Of the plain grey bird
The not-so-little bird
Complete with canted tail
That hops the driveway
And struts the walk

Then I'll be home here
And not before

I don't even know its song

Significant Citing

Two robins
One each
On branch and wire
Orange breasts
To the sun

Oh joy
May I say
Spring I believe
When there was
No winter

On the flyway
Not staying
Not residing here
A turning time
Leaving for home

In every town
All in the past
All those years
Then even here
Robins
Glory

An Ormond Beach Bestiary

Armadillo
Armored, it would seem
Yet vulnerable to cars,
Crushed at the roadside

Butterflies
Monarchs of the air
Or white moths that flutter by
Delight so each spring

Crow
Let's be honest now
You rule when you choose to
Caw all you want to

Deer
They walked down my street
Five abreast, bold, side by side
Long before I came

Egret
Snowy, crooked neck
Denizen of the wet ditch
Your beauty startles

Flicker
Come and get that bug
It's hidden in the oak bark
Drill, kill it, eat

Feral Pigs
The Spanish brought you
Running the deep forest still
Rut, root and trample

Gecko
Amuse every day
Grey on grey to brown on brown
Run the trees, oh please

Heron
Great blue, so beloved
Bird wanted most to be seen
Be here, beside me

Hawk
Soaring way up there
Surveying before the kill
I'm watching you watch

Ibis
Ancient, on the scene
Didn't think I'd see you here
As Egyptians once did

Jay
So loud I'm stunned
You're not just the only one
Has a song to sing

Kestrel
Bird about water
Moving along as tides move
Eating clams today

Land Turtle
Gopher to locals
So determined, yet so slow
Kids watch where you go

Manatee
Good ol' brushy face
We're trying hard to save you
Don't ever leave us

Nuthatch
Not much to say now
When you're in the yard or gone
You "seem" domestic.

Owl
Once I saw you by day
Be wise with hoots and low cries
Granddad of the street

Pelican
Squadron of the beach
Dive down to catch a wave fish
Just beyond our reach

Question
Does some city girl
Old now, with eyes wide open
Have a right to joy?

Roaches
I do not love you
Don't even come in my door
Flip over, feet up, die.

Robin
Spring on the back fence
Come here for rest from the North
Sing out the season

Shrimp
Who would have thunk it
Such bounty, so much plenty
Pull the nets up tight

Turkeys (wild)
First Christmas I came
She marched up my front lawn
An Audubon drawing

Ursus (The Brown Bear)
Here among us now
They're on our turf, we in theirs
Hot tub, tree crotch, yard

Vultures
Nature's dark cleaners
Uglier than sin; wattled
Patrolling for death

Worm (wrestling)
Twist the slatted stick
Make that sound down in the ground
Get ready, go fish

Whales
Haven't seen one here
But some watch from shore and count
At least one this year

X
The X marks the spot
Where the mastodon was found
Just nearby, downtown

Yellow-bellied Sap Sucker
What a claim to fame
I do not wonder at you now
Only at your name

Dream Zebra
Night-dream animal
Prancing about on hard hoofs
I know your bright stripes

WORLD WITHIN

"any kind of knowing that
sets the record straight
gives off a perfumed kind of hope"
(The Naming Before Knowing)

Color Theory

Some suggest the whole rainbow as a remedy.
They surely know color if they say this.
Some suggest the whole rainbow as a remedy.
They would apply the entire spectrum as a cure.

I used the blue-red light once.
I know that one.
I cured my soul with it.
I energized my womb with it.
Deep purple when I used it,
it hummed its blue-red color
until the vibrations became violet
and less powerful, but more lovely
as I recall.

Some suggest the whole rainbow as a remedy,
employing red light for inflammation
and burns that sear the flesh.
Yes, and yellow is good for congestion, they say.
Yellow will make you speak again, when you cannot.
Sit in the yellow of the sun,
you will see, you will sing runs of notes in yellow light
when you could not speak.

And blue is good for insomnia and nervousness.
Blue will satisfy your mind.
It, too, will make you sing,
and the song might be that indigo color
made of part earth and part night.
You would hum the darkness down.
Then you could sleep.

Some suggest the whole rainbow as a cure.
Newton felt that violet had tiny particles,
like so many flowers,
and red was big, like corpuscles.
He might have been wrong, but it was true for him
Red is that big, when you think of it.
Red is blood, there is no denying that.

There are as many kinds of truth
as there are colors,
streaming back like so many flags.
And it takes two, three,
to make each reality whole.

Use color theory.
Spread the rainbow on me.
Divide the light and make me whole.

Poem for Anyone

What if I told you
this wasn't a poem to anyone,
it was just about the night
and longing.

What if I told you
the moon is so waxy big
between blue-grey clouds
that it seems yellow, overripe.

What if I told you
this isn't a poem to anyone,
and the tuber roses smell so strong
their scent is on the walls,

covers the inside
of my mouth
and, of course,
defies logic, knows none.

What if I told you
the moon can
pull me through the walls
on nights like this, a little humid,

a little Southern, as though
my body had too much water
and the walls were a sieve
and I was strained through, purified.

Once the walls of this house
were like that,
made of hollow brick
each was the center of a hive

and the bees ran in the walls
and they slept in the walls
and the honey ran down the walls
of my room, before it was my room.

I can imagine the sweetness
the ooze of it
and the sound of buzzing
in the quiet night.

Last night the moon was full.
It ran between the clouds
so beautifully, the sky was
fish scales and veils.

The rooms filled with moon
the sky was the ocean
and I swam in it
the deep blue of it.

And if I told you all this
in a place where
the sky is blank
and it never rains in summer.

All this in a place
where there are no clouds
yet the breeze is humid now
with longing and a little sadness.

Tonight the moon is a little
past full and far too yellow
for its own good and mine.
The moon is a little off balance, off center.

And if I told you
women are out there
in the streets, wondering
what is different about this night.

What if I told you
this isn't a poem for anyone
it comes from a heart
filled with the moon

Wondering how the moon shines
in another country
when I'm not there.
What if I told you.

Equal Halves

I could cut the world in halves
along its own equator,
loving the imaginary red line as I go.
Or I make quarters and sections of it, not quite equal,
like an orange beneath its bubbled skin.
And yes, again, the world, wobbly,
not exactly as circular
as we supposed,
top-heavy with humanity
weighted down with beliefs and
the human blood of wars, viscous,
with all that hangs heavy at the bottom,
drooping islands of unusual size, Madagascar,
Australia, what was once Ceylon,
pendulous as the precious pearl earrings of the Renaissance.
And all that ice, melted, unmelted,
much more than is at the top.

I could cut an apple in halves down the mid-line
but the sections are not equal,
pips and core and stem obscure the true center
and guide me away from the plumb line.
I only intuit with my knife.
So, I measure the parts by eye,
giving you the smaller half,
passing it to you elegantly,
telling you it is the larger one.
Saying, "If you eat that, it will be more than enough."
ls it? Not by half.

And, of course, there is the brain,
seemingly symmetrical in its enfolding,
but not.
Some centers so used that they are worth their weight
the halves connected by a rubbery bridge,
to be crossed when possible.
My mother's brain
burned by strokes and zaps,
hundreds of electrical incidents,
big ones, little ones.
It was never equal to begin with,
leaning as it did to emotion and song — all tilted,
destroyed tiny continent by continent.

Then, myself.
Far beyond the crisis of mid-life wanting,
desiring more than half of everything, everyone.
Some would call me middle-aged now,
but I know better, listening for balance
in the quiet I have acquired.
If this were the middle, now,
equally divided along memory and expectation,
I would live beyond the biblical span allotted,
Five score and twenty.
As it is, I am now two-thirds of my grandmother's 99
without her strength of will and ability to terrorize.
I am closer to the end now than I would have thought,
all thoughts being equal.

The Braid, The Cap of Hair
— *for women walking away*

Recently, I have come to find out
that at Auschwitz there are bales of hair,
mostly Jewish women's hair, shorn,
saved by the Nazis, for some hideous purpose
it was then saved by us, for the rest of us.
It has been photographed, documented,
because it disintegrates about now,
falling to dust and nothing,
long after the heads it covered
are dust and nothing.
It informs everything
that I know of myself
and who I have come to be
and how I am alive.

What is to be done with all this hair?
To destroy it now could be considered
desecration.
To destroy it now
could be to deny the past
and we have said, we will never,
never deny the past, never forget.
Never again,
women torn from their husbands,
their children.
Women waiting in line for water
that is poisoned air.

Women waiting to be baked, thrown in pits,
their rings piled up, their clothes neatly folded,
piled. Their hair in bales.

We know our own truth.
The past doesn't die.
The power of memory doesn't die.
We carry it as a weapon,
A covering of modesty.

Grandma
you sat bald beneath some strands of silver hair.
You sat tied
so you will not run on legs
that could not walk
and you live each moment again
in some crazy order only you understand.
Now 1908, now 1893, 1983.
You spoke Russian again.
You shout Yiddish
and wonder
"Where are the children,
Kinder, vas tust du?"
Why aren't they home for supper
And the table laid?

Grandma, we cut our reddish hair
As you did, in defiance, in practicality.
We make a cap, a helmet of it
to face the world.
We cut our hair
to define our world.

We paint it blond,
we shave it close
in sorrow, in rage,
because we see death
or know an anger so red
we can do nothing else.

I have considered smoothing the entire head to bone
to lose the world, the Buddhist way,
and find it.
I had considered what the women of my world have done,
shaving it close, to be a Chassid
as your grandmothers were, mothers were,
and have their place of modesty secure
within a tiny universe,
wearing another's hair.

We cut our hair
or lose it to a death-defying cocktail.
We wrap our heads with scarves
we deceive the world
into believing a modesty we do not have.

In death
hair grows
nails grow.
Our dreams live on in other people's minds.

When we dance our hair flutters out
streams behind us, or shakes in waves
and curlicues.
As a child, my sister's hair so curled
around itself
I could not put my fingers through it.
It was its own universe of knots.

Seeing the brain just beneath the skull
as a walnut
doesn't always keep me in my right mind.
I slide away from knowing
what I have always known,
pretending I don't walk
the convoluted line
that is the braid of women's truth.

Grandma's braid,
red and twisted, is in the Bible
on the shelf in the living room
no longer there.
309 South Lotus, Chicago, Illinois.
I see it, I smell it,
like powder.
When some women cut off the past
they save it.
Stored at the heart's core,
it is stuffed into quilts
twisted as memento mori into lockets,
braided around wrists,
held as children of men no longer loved.
When women cut off the past
to seem to emancipate their lives
they keep memory beneath a cap of hair.

And we are all bound together
as in a braid, twisted close.
All of us, those I love,
my daughter,
more wild and delicate than myself.

But we are loosening our lives, letting go
and sitting back to back
slowly unbraiding the love
waiting for the braid to loosen,
without unbraiding,
with the pain of sitting still,
not moving away.
Although our backs are turned
we are bound together
though we move apart.

Though we leave, always,
each other, pull apart
disguised as women of the world
disguised as warriors,
hausfraus,
little girls with braids behind our backs,
we are not apart from any.
We remain, woven together
webbed out along
an almost imaginary line
some celestial hairnet.
Some cosmic union of filaments
like those of the Goddess Nut,
purchased at a five-and-dime of memory
a place of icons for sale
within any woman's reach.

And though we turn to leave
and though we turn away
From everything we were
we cannot.

We are caught in memory
held close
as with a cap of hair.

Of course, there is the power of all this.
There is the knowledge that when
Phaedra prepared to love a boy
she should not love,
she loosed one pin
that held her elegant coif aloft
and all that hair fell down along her back,
cascaded really,
and no boy, no man
could resist her,
no matter what his innocence.

And there is the fear that when I moved
from him whom I had fiercely loved
the hairs would tear from my head,
turn white, exposing me.
And nothing would cover
the death that dream,
so I screamed myself awake.

Knowing these things,
and other secret women's thoughts
of who we are, generation after generation,
light sometimes abounds,
shapes haloes out beyond my head,
makes shards of yellow light
that pierce the inner eye.

The Naming Before Knowing

That's how it mostly is
with me these days,
humped over my own pain
clomping around on bloody stumps
clapping without palms
grasping without so much
as a thumb
to hook into things.

Ah, but now,
now I've seen Chaos.
I can name her
and everything is changed.
She becomes like a sister to me.
They have drawn her for me,
those wily scientists who can do
those things I just imagine.
They have made traceable her wings
shimmering with variables
beating out their mad
exquisite pattern, pattern upon pattern
like a heart about to wear itself
into infinity.

Well, yes,
right now, that kind of knowing
any kind of knowing that
sets the record straight
gives off a perfumed kind of hope.

Adam knew that. He knew
he had the terrible responsibility
to name almost everything.
And when you can almost
name the unnamable,
the ineffable,
or at least sense its shape
next to you, like sheltering dark wings,
it gives a kind of
momentary peace.

Adam knew that —
the first namer,
he went East of Eden.

This Is A Bowl

This is a bowl
It holds my heart for meat
It was fired with fire
And the glaze is ash

This is a basket
Made from my nerves
Entwined

This is a cup
Full of liquid thought
Drink me

This is a bag of skin
Hear my bones within
Rattle and knock

This is a vessel
Of unknown origin
Perhaps it is me entire
Filled with what I am

This is a box postpaid
Sending me to you

Receive it

Transit of Venus

Oh to be a nipple on the sun
To be observed
Around the world
The masculine gaze upon you
Sensuous yet dangerous
Like the breast of life
Never to be looked at
Directly
A kind of lewd thing
Forbidden, injurious
To the onlooker

Shield your eyes
Look away from this beauty
And the awesome manifestations
Of what is
Womanly power

Indigo Girl

I'm the indigo girl
The third-eye gal
Safe in the cosmos' pocket
Held closed with a pin

All seeing all knowing
I weep and laugh at it all
And because of it
I can do no less

Don't cross me now
I'm the devil's cousin
Your arguments are useless
No matter what

I'm the poker player's
Daughter/wife
One-eyed Jack's my uncle
Queen of hearts my mama

What's canasta to do with me
Straw hats by the pool
Cigars during 4-handed games
In the *shvitch* locker room

Consider the options
Hold 'em—fold 'em
Go all in
Being me myself
Go all in

At the Counter

At the counter
Day or nite
Things happen
That do not happen
At a table

The disabled dishwasher
Talks incessantly
To the hot stack
Of plates and bowls
He places neatly
The sentient beings
That they are

The kitchen help
Hair like Rasta men
Have their very own
Patois and rhythm
They move and groove
Turning that perfect pancake
While doing the kitchen dance

Waitresses slide in
Reminding adding
They laugh and dance a little
Saying, "outrageous, you guys"
While pleased

It is all easy side by side
And forwards with a smile
They can call you "honey"
Not thinking it demeaning
After all, you're a regular

RESILIENCE

"There is an ache in the human heart
a yearning to transform all dross and suffering to joy
matched only in the dark hearts of stars."
(*Dark Hearts of Stars*)

-

The Dark Hearts of Stars

There is an ache in the human heart,
a yearning to transform all dross and suffering to joy,
matched only in the dark hearts of stars.

In the heated alchemy of stellar change,
a power that has no name and no intention,
so like the power of unquestioning love,
turns lead to gold
though human science once could not.

As huge stars explode, within their centers
lead and what is base turn to precious metals
and are flung out into the universe
so far and how very, very far,
making a light we see and celebrate
a thousand thousand years beyond that time.

As we glance out at the night sky
we come to know the history of the universe in an instant
thrilled with vision and some understanding.

And, then, again, as we turn to our beloved,
we, too, are transformed,
it is as if we have become the cauldron
that is the dark hearts of stars.
For, in the instant, there is a force of love so powerful
that dark stars themselves explode within,
making of self a stellar incandescence,
lit by a power beyond itself.

What Hope Is Like

This is what hope is like
I should know
It's the color yellow
The first bite of bitter chocolate
The warm smell of a man's arm
But hope is ridiculous
Especially when
It is all there is
Not derision
Nor disdain
Which is sour

But hope is yellow
Yellow even in
Morning sunlight
Or like harvest moon glow
Reflected
Remember
Bitter chocolate
Holds a promise
Of sweetness
Just as you bite
This is hope

Remember the smell
Of a man's arm
As it was
Holding drinks
Holding clubs
Or fountain pens

To miss someone
It is not the same as hope
And I want hope now
Give me that
I deserve it
I hunger for it

The One-Way Truck

Bring everything here
Leave it
Dump it
I'll arrange it

Bring every goddamn thing
Things we should have sold
Heavy things
Things that will rust
Things that explode on arrival
(Don't ask)
Things that fall down and break

Bring it
Bring yourself
Already too damaged to survive
Still lookin' good while rotting away
Broken at the broken parts
Already

Drop it
Offload the weight
The vital organs
The skin
Drop it
Leave it be
I'll arrange it

We the Living

It is not required to die
To know death
Sit by sit by
Look death in the eye
Hear it rasp down
To nothingness
Still warm

If you know all this
And choose to go on
Then do go on
Go ahead
Advancing retreating
Seeing the world
Through blued rain-streaked
Windows

The future trails vapors
Of the silent past
Pictures darkening
On screens of the mind
We will never forget
We have already forgotten

Each Caregiver Prays

Each caregiver prays
To their own God
Almost all to Christ
I am sure

One listens to new gospel
More like rap than prayer
One reads the Bible
Taking notes, copious notes
To write and then transcribe
Another talks out loud to God
Each and every night
So sure God listens
Especially when she sleeps

You see how it is
And this is not all
Because none prays for me
Except one
For me not to be a Jew
Only for Christ to save me
Not for me to save myself

As I am

God's Ugly Children

Of God's ugly children
Surely I have become one
Blasted, bifurcated
Destroyed from within
Mean with pain
Going on despite

No vestigial wings to lift
No prehensile tail to grab
Practically naked without
The fur we all once had

Standing here amazed
Undone, splayed top down
Waiting to be emptied out
Or mended by methods yet
Unknown

Perhaps a little smile still
Around the rheumy eyes
Perhaps a little grieving
For what could have been
The beauty and the grace

Hello Foot

Oh hello foot
Bone of my leg
Welcome to my mouth
Fibula to face
Amazing
Amazing transforming
Reconstruction
Of self by self

Transplant transformation
Transubstantiation
For me to become me again
Old and yet so young
Reborn
In my hopes for my life
Renewed

I Offer You the Comfort

I offer you the comfort of my shoulder
No, not that shoulder, the other one
I offer you the comfort of my breast
To rest your head upon
Not as a mother
But as a would-be lover
Too old now to offer more
The body as evidence
Of what I have to give

Take what you can
Although you hesitate
No need to reciprocate
Each gesture I make to you
You have already given more
More to me
Than I would ever ask

Just receive what little I offer
I ask nothing
But to give you comfort
When I can

Nurse Lunni's Quilt

I have brought home
Nurse Lunni's quilt
A blanket of care
To cover me each night

Soft and warm
A little smile, a calming glance
A hummed piece
Of a Jesus tune

She will sit outside my room
All night if I need her
She will walk the halls at midnight
If I am anxious and I need to

I have brought her quiet, caring spirit home

Song Without Words

No witty repartee
No recital on the stage today
Song above the eyebrows
Sung inside of me

Nothing on the tongue today
Tomorrow maybe
No minor keys
To sing the song inside of me

Words Have Gotten Thin

Words have gotten thin
Shatter like ice
But do not melt
Shards shards
Fragments everywhere

Words have gotten thin
Strong winds blow through them
Sea sounds and whale sounds
Not human sounds at all

Words have gotten thin
I trace their shadows
On the walls of my skull
Recollect what they once were
Memories of utterances once made

SOURCES

Rosella Stern's daughter Rebecca Bloom has given permission to publish any or all of Rosella's poetry.

Unpublished poems are from Rosella's papers.

12 Trends to Watch Comes November is a collection of twelve poems printed and copyrighted by Rosella in 1993 in Seattle Washington.

If Not Now - West Coast Poems was published in 2012 by Xlibris Corporation.

Preliminary Kaddish was published in 2015 by Writers Ink Press, Daytona Beach Florida.

52 Pickup – A Pack of Poems was printed and copyrighted by Rosella in 2020.

ON WRITING
"Gimme a Chunka Thick White Paper" (Originally written between 1969 and 1970, unpublished)

"These Poems!" (Originally written between 1969 and 1970, unpublished)

"Comes November" (Reprinted from *12 Trends to Watch Comes November* 1993 and *If Not Now: West Coast Poems* 2012)

"Psalms for Today" (Reprinted from *52 Pickup – A Pack of Poems* 2020)

"A Thought So Grievous" (Reprinted from *52 Pickup – A Pack of Poems* 2020)

"What the Old Man Told Me" (Reprinted from *52 Pickup – A Pack of Poems* 2020)

"One O'Clock Revision" (Reprinted from *52 Pickup – A Pack of Poems* 2020)

"Poetry in Motion" (Originally written in Seattle between 1987 and 2008, reprinted from *If Not Now: West Coast Poems* 2012)

REMEMBERING
"The Snow Prince – For my father dead a dozen years" (Originally written in 1986, unpublished)

"Tending Beauty, the Rose and the Thorn" (Originally written in Seattle between 1987 and 2008, reprinted from *If Not Now: West Coast Poems*)

"Our Mother's Daughters" (Originally written in Seattle between 1987 and 2008, reprinted from *If Not Now: West Coast Poems* 2012)

"For Buby" (Originally written in 1989 as a eulogy for Rosella's grandmother, Dora Strunin Rein Gold, unpublished)

"Cutting Bread" (Originally written in Seattle between 1987 and 2008, reprinted from *If Not Now: West Coast Poems* 2012)

"Backyard Shadow" (Reprinted from *52 Pickup – A Pack of Poems* 2020)

"Backyard Girls" (Unpublished, date unknown)

YIDDISH SOUL
"If I Believe – At the Jewish New Year" (Originally written in

Seattle between 1987 and 2008, reprinted from *If Not Now: West Coast Poems* 2012)

"The Eight Ways of Giving" (Originally written in Seattle between 1987 and 2008, reprinted from *If Not Now: West Coast Poems* 2012)

"Prohibitions Sacred and Profane" (Reprinted from *52 Pickup – A Pack of Poems* 2020)

"The Sweet Smoke of Prayer" (Reprinted from *52 Pickup – A Pack of Poems* 2020)

"Fearing the Smallest of Small Things" (Reprinted from *52 Pickup – A Pack of Poems* 2020)

"Need to Breathe" (Unpublished, date unknown)

"Biblical Magic" (Reprinted from *52 Pickup – A Pack of Poems* 2020)

"Seven Yiddish Curses for Today" (Unpublished draft 2018)

LOVE AND LOSS
"The Dying Heart" (Reprinted from *Preliminary Kaddish* 2015)

"Sorrow's Half" (Originally published in *Preliminary Kaddish* 2015. Reprinted from an edited version in *52 Pickup – A Pack of Poems* 2020)

"Shoes and Paperwork" (Reprinted from *Preliminary Kaddish* 2015)

"The Absence of Blackness" (Reprinted from *Preliminary Kaddish* 2015)

"The Anatomy of Tear" (Reprinted from *Preliminary Kaddish* 2015)

"Future Nostalgia" (Reprinted from *Preliminary Kaddish* 2015)

"Ain't Gonna Use Black Magic on It" (Originally written in San Diego between 1983 and 1986, reprinted from *If Not Now: West Coast Poems* 2012)

"Him" (Reprinted from *52 Pickup – A Pack of Poems* 2020)

"Glass Can Cut Glass" (Originally written in San Diego between 1983 and 1986, reprinted from *If Not Now: West Coast Poems* 2012)

"What is Air" (Unpublished, date unknown)

"Do You Know Darkness" (Originally written in San Diego between 1983 and 1986, reprinted from *If Not Now: West Coast Poems* 2012)

"Red Wagon" (Originally written in Seattle between 1987 and 2008, reprinted from *If Not Now: West Coast Poems* 2012)

OBSERVATIONS
"The Mystery of the Ordinary" (Reprinted from *Preliminary Kaddish* 2015)

"The Hawks" (Reprinted from *Preliminary Kaddish* 2015)

"The Crows Will Have a Use for It" (Reprinted from *52 Pickup – A Pack of Poems* 2020)

"A Minyan of Ibis" (Reprinted from *52 Pickup – A Pack of Poems* 2020)

"Orion" (Reprinted from *52 Pickup – A Pack of Poems* 2020)

"Southern Birds" (Reprinted from *52 Pickup – A Pack of Poems* 2020)

"Significant Citing" (Reprinted from *52 Pickup – A Pack of Poems* 2020)

"An Ormond Beach Bestiary" (Draft 2018)

WORLD WITHIN
"Color Theory" (Originally written in San Diego between 1983 and 1986, reprinted from *12 Trends to Watch Comes November* 1993 and *If Not Now: West Coast Poems* 2012)

"Poem for Anyone" (Originally written in San Diego between 1983 and 1986, reprinted from *If Not Now: West Coast Poems* 2012)

"Equal Halves" (Originally written in Seattle between 1987 and 2008, reprinted from *If Not Now: West Coast Poems* 2012)

"The Braid, The Cap of Hair – For Women Walking Away" (This poem was originally printed as its own book by Bellevue Community College Women's Center, Bellevue, Washington 1994. It was later edited and printed in *If Not Now: West Coast Poems* 2012. The edited version is reprinted in this publication, *Rosella*.)

"The Naming Before Knowing" (Originally written in Seattle between 1987 and 2008, reprinted from *12 Trends to Watch Comes November* 1993 and *If Not Now: West Coast Poems* 2012)

"This is a Bowl" (Reprinted from *52 Pickup – A Pack of Poems* 2020)

"Transit of Venus" (Reprinted from *52 Pickup – A Pack of Poems* 2020)

"Indigo Girl" (Reprinted from *52 Pickup – A Pack of Poems* 2020)

"At the Counter" (Reprinted from *52 Pickup – A Pack of Poems* 2020)

RESILIENCE
"The Dark Hearts of Stars" (Originally written in Seattle between 1987 and 2008, reprinted from *If Not Now: West Coast Poems* 2012)

"What Hope Is Like" (Reprinted from *52 Pickup – A Pack of Poems* 2020)

"The One-Way Truck" (Reprinted from *52 Pickup – A Pack of Poems* 2020)

"We the Living" (Reprinted from *52 Pickup – A Pack of Poems* 2020)

"Each Care Giver Prays" (Written 2022, unpublished)

'God's Ugly Children" (Written 2021, unpublished)

"Hello Foot" (Written 2021, unpublished)

"I Offer You the Comfort" (Written 2022, unpublished)

"Nurse Lunni's Quilt" (Written 2021, unpublished)

"Song Without Words" (Written 2021, unpublished)

"Words Have Gotten Thin" (Written 2021, unpublished)